Mint Snowball

Books by Naomi Shihab Nye

Poetry
Different Ways to Pray
Hugging the Jukebox
Yellow Glove
Red Suitcase
Words Under the Words: Selected Poems
The Spoken Page
Fuel

Poetry for Young Readers — Editor
This Same Sky, A Collection of Poems from Around the World
The Tree is Older than You Are
I Feel a Little Jumpy Around You
(co-edited with Paul B. Janeczko)
The Space Between Our Footsteps:
Poems & Paintings from the Middle East
What Have You Lost?
Salting the Ocean

Picture Books
Sitti's Secrets
Benito's Dream Bottle
Lullaby Raft
Come With Me: Poems for a Journey

Novel for Teens
Habibi

Essays
Never in a Hurry

Chapbooks
Mint
Invisible
The Miracle of Typing
Eye-to-Eye
Tattooed Feet

Mint Snowball

Naomi Shihab Nye

Anhinga Press, 2001
Tallahassee, Florida

Cover art
Paula Owen – *Lawn*, 1998

Cover design, book design and production – Lynne Knight

Library of Congress Cataloging-in-Publication Data
Mint Snowball by Naomi Shihab Nye – First Edition
ISBN 0938078-68-2
Library of Congress Card Number: 00-110509

*This publication is sponsored in part by a grant from the Florida Department
of State, Division of Cultural Affairs, and the Florida Arts Council.*

Anhinga Press Inc. is a nonprofit corporation dedicated wholly
to the publication and appreciation of fine poetry.
For personal orders, catalogs and information write to:
Anhinga Press
P.O. Box 3665
Tallahassee, FL 32315
Web site: www.anhinga.org
E-mail: info@anhinga.org

Published in the United States by Anhinga Press, Tallahassee, Florida.
First Edition, 2001

*With gratitude
to Judith Kitchen*

Contents

Deep Time

Piecemeal Lives

Sunday Newspaper

Appetite

Epilogue

Acknowledgments

I am grateful to the places some of these pieces first appeared: *Paragraph, The Tampa Review, The Prose Poem: An International Journal, In Short,* edited by Judith Kitchen and Mary Paumier Jones (W.W. Norton & Co., 1996), *Five Points, Luna,* and *The Midwest Quarterly.*

The title piece first appeared in *Never in a Hurry: Essays on People & Places,* by Naomi Shihab Nye (University of South Carolina Press, 1996) and is reprinted with their permission.

"How to Get There" was first read on National Public Radio.

Mint Snowball

Deep Time

From Earth

… comes the bleeding berry, reaching arm of tomato, twisted vine. I promise you. First there will be dirt, then a shining line of corn tassels, neighborhood of grapes, burgeoning jewels. All from the ground up. *And who are you among them?* Reach in through prickly leaves to slice the stem. The boys I worked with lived across the black/white line in the borough that only grown-ups could see. First time we'd met. *May I use your knife?* We poured water over each other's hands. Years later no line but an edginess in a few voices. *Where did the neighborhood go?* Oh! Not one house is missing. You can know what makes a plant easier than a person. To carry squash in a bucket. Human in relation to corn. Human in relation to empty bushel baskets stacked in barn. Human in relation to husk. *And what will you say years later when they keep asking you why you're attracted to "ordinary objects"?* Even before I worked on the farm, my mother pulled us down the hill in a wagon, tomatoes stacked in our laps. The seed of that early someone must travel in me now, flicker of light still shaping, tiny as an echo poured through a pipe — *what will you make make make of your lives?*

Job

My father did not want me to work at the farm. Good thing I had a mother too. Rumble in the living room. I told the farmers I would be at work on Monday. Al never got excited unless somebody drove over his hose when the water was on.

On Monday I knelt with strawberries. Knees of my pants grew muddy and wet. Later we plucked blackberries wearing cans on ropes around our necks. Fingertips stained inky dark. Careful not to bruise the berries. Each night, a new primary berry declared itself, soaking up the dark sky, ready for picking by morning. So much happened in silence on the farm. Caroline arranged the berries in stained pint boxes in the back of the truck. Now when someone drove up the driveway and honked a horn, she could fill their order. I wanted to pick more and more and more. You could become addicted to picking. But Caroline shrieked, "That's enough!" You could become addicted to weeding too. Something clicked inside your mind. By one we were stunned with heat, trudging home downhill, glory of jingling nickels, bumblebees buzzing a crack in the barn. Making their own world we couldn't see.

Thirty-four years later I kneel in the same exact field. The strawberries have moved up a bit. Al drags a hoe down freshly tilled earth. Rows open. I measure the space between cucumber seeds. Our 12-year-old son beside me. Same age I was then. Same folks telling us what to do. I never imagined "coming back" so exactly. All this time, I was only a day and a half away from childhood. By road. The farmers were still here, picking, canning, weeding, listening to the radio deep into the night, never leaving ... they could have used the help.

Translated, transported, deep time shimmering under the skin of so many days. Far off calling kids. Where our voices used to be. Consider the word "still" in all its rich dimensions. Engines, motors, secret oasis inside city limits. *Where the ants crawled into my lunch sack. Where the boy stood when he asked if my father lived in a tent* ... deep time trembles and sweats. *Who?* When Al asks me to move my car, I have to think for a moment. *Can I drive?*

The Mind of Squash

Overnight, and quietly. Beneath the scratchy leaf we thicken and expand so fast you can't believe. Sun pours into us. We drink midnight too, blue locust lullaby feeding our graceful sleep. When you come back, we are fat. Doubled in the dark. Faster than you are. Sometimes we grow together, two of us twining out from the same stalk, conversational blossoms. Bring the bucket. Bring the small knife with the sharp blade. Bring the wind to cool our wide span of leaves, each one bigger than a human head, bigger than dinner plates. Wait till you find the giant prize we have hidden from you all along — no muscle-rich upper arm exceeds its size. But the farmer doesn't like it. Too big for selling, he says. Only for zucchini bread. Never mind. We like it. We have our own pride.

Shade

Are these the same trees or the children of the trees that used to be here? Nothing changes space more than trees. They rest us. At dusk, exhausted and streaked with dirt, we sit beneath trees with slices of melon. We joke. We sing. I never knew the farmer liked to sing till we got old and he told me. Why would you hide this from a child? Singing was his hope. In my family when people did not get what they wanted, they walked out a door and stared at the horizon. They sang too. My mother sang in English and my father sang in Arabic. They disappeared for awhile or trimmed a tree with long clippers. Better than hitting. Better than cursing or drinking, I guess. I sat in the cool den under pine trees between my house and Barbara's house. The farmer's grandfather used to own our street, too. Our street was once part of the farm. When I find Barbara this trip, she says, "I don't remember you so much. I remember your brother." I would hike to the farm. Talk to trees along the way. Tell them our troubles. I bought lima beans for my mother and Caroline folded the top of the bag so neatly. As if she didn't have thousands of things to do.

Junk

He never threw one bit or scrap of anything away. The metal, the rivet, the sack. Unread newspapers stacked on the ends of the bed. Is it a shield, an armor? Is it something about not being lonesome in the future? Is it a fear? The farmer surrounds himself with wire, glass jars, shoeboxes, crates. And what does he think he will do with it all?

Receipts. Rope. Open any barn door, the barn is *stuffed*. Open any shed. *What would you do with a husband like that?* She herds me into the living room when he's out with the corn. Passageway a foot wide between mounds of junk piled to the ceiling. *Kick his butt.* I can't believe I said "butt" to someone from my childhood. Fireplace they can't reach. Stairway to the second floor totally jammed. *Did you even know we had a second floor?* One million editions of *Organic Gardening* magazine. *Prevention.* She would have liked to have furniture like any regular person. Places to sit. *Do you see now why I don't give a damn?* Empty vitamin bottles dating back to the fifties. The wide sadness of the world comes sweeping through, sadness of the impossible grip, my grandfather unwrapping soaps so they would harden and last longer, right up till he died.

I Was Thinking of Poems

In the fields our eyes whirled inside a blur of green. Before I
wore glasses I came here. Thought the world was soft at the
far edges for real. Green rim of trees alongside anyone's life.
Stalk. Pod. Tendril. Blossom. On a farm you had time. Your
mind on words. Turned over gently and longly inside your
head. Damp dirt under dry surface.

He said "Rain" or "Easy." Said "String" or "Yellow." A boy
said "Yes sir" but meant "I don't get it." A phrase dangled.
Strip of cloud. Wide angle. Line breaks. Where the asparagus
row turned into the beets.

What Happened to Everybody

Lodholz, Schwendener, Bauer, Kraft. The one who was thin got fat and the one who was fat, athletic. So many Chinese restaurants! Now there is a walking tour. Historical buildings. Douglas went into oil. He moved to Houston and his parents do not remember me though their son has appeared in more than one of my writings. They don't look happy to hear this. *By name?* they say. *You said his name?* Schoolyard swoon: 120 years of echoing kids. I find my spot behind a tree. In a trashcan, "My Personal Dictionary" hand-lettered by Eric. Open to L: *Look, Love, Live, Lose, Listen, Light.* Everything he needed right there on one page — how could he throw it away? My friend Marsha lives in her parents' house. Show me the laundry chute. The bulletin board. The room where we played Parcheesi with our brothers on a low coffee table while our parents discussed business in the living room. The Canadians split up. The Italians moved west. Many people disappeared entirely, though their porch steps retain the same chips and cracks. *Here is the ditch where I lost my blue sewing thread. The house we were scared of. The auto body shop. The grocery store where my brother dropped a watermelon so they would give it to us free.* Missy and her father put Missy's mother into a nursing home (*she wasn't even sick*) then flew off to Europe. They sent postcards back to the neighbors, who never mentioned when they visited Missy's mother what a great time Missy and her dad were having.

She could have gone too. Why would you do that to your own mother? They went on to Cairo to see the pyramids, their biggest dream. Missy's father fell over dead at the foot of the Sphinx and was brought home in a coffin. The neighbors swear he looked positively Egyptian.

Mint

We all grew mint in patches in our yards, my father and
mother, uncles, aunts. Passing rooted sprigs to neighbors,
crowning summer jugs of lemonade as Greeks and Romans
once crowned themselves with mint leaves. In some yards the
mint spiralled out of flower beds or flourished where the air
conditioner dripped. My parents snipped it up for salads. I
liked to arrange bouquets of mint in juice glasses next to the
sink. It made the room feel fresh. Once my two uncles were
fighting near the mint bed, socking each other with their
fists, and one ripped the other's shirt open so his buttons
popped off into the grass. My mother shouted, "Oh! — Oh!
— Oh!" Later we were kneeling, looking for buttons, while
they sat at the kitchen table laughing,
drinking tea with mint.

Not Even a Story

When the last great-uncle dies, we inherit a box of letters
written in graceful script on paper so rich you could drink it.
Nothing is like this anymore. We have lost handwriting, we
have lost the art of the perfectly indented address. I meet a
whole crowd of Germans telling about the two-headed neigh-
bor baby, the run-away cart, the elopement, the birthday roast.
The letter in which my great-grandmother told my great-
grandfather she could never, never under any circumstances,
marry him. What happened next? They had seven children
together, only one of whom would ever marry. They moved to
Portland. They rode a train across the country with a week-old
baby. I stack the letters in sequences. In 1893 great-great-
uncle John accepted a call to be minister in Philo, Illinois. He
had so much to do he didn't know where to begin. He sat
in his study and despaired. Expected to visit everybody in his
congregation regularly and stay for meals, he wrote, "I never
did find much pleasure in visiting, but now it seems to be out
of me entirely." He rattled around in a house of five rooms.
He traveled by cart on a deeply rutted road. Visiting people
made him feel lonelier. He got so lonesome "not even a story"
could afford him pleasure. Suddenly I know what I am doing
in my life. I am collecting stories for great-great-uncle John. I
am trying them out on his dead ear. Leaning up against him in
the atmosphere, saying, "Isn't this a little better than nothing
was?" I am lifting up his glum Lutheran fear.

Nice Place to Live

Sometimes she drives by her own old-fashioned house cast-
ing a glance left, curving front porch, white pillars, shaded
purple swing, lavish queen's crown vine climbing southern
wall, pouring pink cascades, hordes of snout-nosed butterflies
swarming blossoms, the profusion, the wild tangle, banana
palms, miniature chiles, blue painted front door through
which many people have certainly walked. What about
the black iron gate held closed by a shoestring? Well, they
couldn't be snobs, that's for sure.

Signs

Once we announced them from the back seat – SERVING
THE HOT DOG WITH DIGNITY – huge hand-painted ochre
letters on a shack with a crooked door. *Stop the car!* I used
to shout. But I had shouted it so often, for doughnut stands
and riverboats, libraries, Arabic grocers, parks with benches,
organ grinders, that we passed on by, I would never know
what that tasted like. Down the block we could have had
– BRAINS 25 cents DRIVE IN – I used to think of them
when I was at school. Now in St. Louis I feel wounded by
apartment buildings, boards slapped over windows. I want
to pitch a tent in any burned-out lot begging blades of grass
to remember us between the ashes. I don't expect to see, but
suddenly, the sharp orange spark gone out of them, softly,
softly they sing, WITH DIGNITY, though the door gapes,
though the roof touches the ground. Where is the sweet lost
grease in the lot studded with coils from demolished heaters?
What gets swallowed by ice and sun, each hope discovering
its tender edge, family businesses that didn't make it, the
Chinese couple selling dozens of salt shakers in their yard.
And the worlds we come to, far from our first ground …
now I live in Texas where the sign offers – T N T BARBEQUE
TERRIBLE DELICIOUS – and I whirl by, biting down on this
terrible delicious air.

The Urge for Epasote

Just because she overhears someone say how pinto beans are no good without it, suddenly she has to have some too. Even though she never heard of it before. What it might be to live without such longings she imagines as the sadness before people kill themselves. Visits grocery stores till at last a small packet of dried in the Tex-Mex market where you spin a roulette wheel to find out if you get your groceries free. Makes beans, dumps in whole packet, eats. And not even memorable. Nothing like cilantro was, first time. Later in Mexico, living in a house with an epasote bush flourishing outside the door, starts putting it fresh in everything till she knows, *knows* what that woman meant. Opposite of dull. But you have to teach your tongue. Tongue has to want it on its own. It can't be *mental.* Back home she finds a single small pot of epasote tucked in among basils and lavenders at the nursery, plants it in ground, waters till it grows bigger than a horse stall. Wind galloping through jaggedy leaves. Lets it go to seed. Gives it to people who never heard of it either. To a young chef, with recipes. Stalks as long as arms, *grow into this.* Tied bundles, string. And keeps her ears open. Next thing you know.

Mint Snowball

My great-grandfather on my mother's side ran a drugstore in a small town in central Illinois. He sold pills and rubbing alcohol from behind the big cash register and creamy ice cream from the soda fountain. My mother remembers the counter's long polished sweep, its shining face. She twirled on the stools. Dreamy fans. Wide summer afternoons. Clink of nickels in anybody's hand. He sold milkshakes, cherry cokes, old-fashioned sandwiches. What did an old-fashioned sandwich look like? Dark wooden shelves. Silver spigots on chocolate dispensers.

My great-grandfather had one specialty: a Mint Snowball which he invented. Some people drove all the way in from Decatur just to taste it. First he stirred fresh mint leaves with sugar and secret ingredients in a small pot on the stove for a very long time. He concocted a flamboyant elixir of mint. Its scent clung to his fingers even after he washed his hands. Then he shaved ice into tiny particles and served it mounded in a glass dish. Permeated with mint syrup. Scoops of rich vanilla ice cream to each side. My mother took a bite of minty ice and ice cream mixed together. The Mint Snowball tasted like winter. She closed her eyes to see the Swiss village my great-grandfather's parents came from. Snow frosting the roofs. Glistening, dangling spokes of ice.

Before my great-grandfather died, he sold the recipe for the mint syrup to someone in town for $100. This hurt my grandfather's feelings. My grandfather thought he should have inherited it to carry on the tradition. As far as the family knew, the person who bought the recipe never used it. At least not in public. My mother had watched her grandfather make the syrup so often she thought she could replicate it.

But what did he have in those little unmarked bottles? She experimented. Once she came close. She wrote down what she did. Now she has lost the paper.

Perhaps the clue to my entire personality connects to the lost Mint Snowball. I have always felt out-of-step with my environment, disjointed in the modern world. The crisp flush of cities makes me weep. Strip centers, poodle grooming and take-out Thai. I am angry over lost department stores, wistful for something I have never tasted or seen.

Although I know how to do everything one needs to know — change airplanes, find my exit off the interstate, charge gas, send a fax — there is something missing. Perhaps the stoop of my great-grandfather over the pan, the slow patient swish of his spoon. The spin of my mother on the high stool with her whole life in front of her, something fine and fragrant still to happen. When I breathe a handful of mint, even pathetic sprigs from my sunbaked Texas earth, I close my eyes. Little chips of ice on the tongue, their cool slide down. Can we follow the long river of the word "refreshment" back to its spring? Is there another land for me? Can
I find any lasting solace in the color green?

Piecemeal Lives

Trouble with Spanish

Each word seems familiar: *limpia, bastante, segundo, planchar*. So it's easy to nod, hearing them — we've met before on this planet of words. If I think a moment, I may remember how or why. But the person who's talking talks faster. I miss all the little links. A car careening down a Mexico City boulevard, skimming past lights, intersections, so each breath becomes a shrine that might say *Si* to anything, or *Bueno*, the optimist's happy raft floating crazily on these wild waves. It may not save me, but I'm hanging on to it, with my deceptively confident rolling *R* and my threadbare Arabic, that likes to sneak into Spanish sentences whenever it can, as if, as if, it all went together, these fragments of language, these piecemeal lives.

How to Get There

At 7 a.m. a driver from a car service comes to collect me on the drizzly upper east side of Manhattan, where I'm a house-guest. I need to go to Paterson, New Jersey, to stomp around with junior high school students for the day. *Paterson, New Jersey, please,* I say. And the driver with his beautiful accent says, *Tell me, how do you get to New Jersey?* Is he kidding? I live in Texas. I know how to get from San Antonio to San Angelo. Obviously we must cross a bridge or traverse a tunnel to go from Manhattan to Jersey, but which one? Beats me. *Call your office,* I say. He doesn't have a phone in the vehicle.

So I urge him, *Pull over* and find myself trumpeting out the window, *How do we get to New Jersey?* at every third corner. No one looks surprised. Lean Latino men step closer to help us. Sleepy grandmas point damp newspapers. And they know. They all know something. If we don't speak to strangers — what will we do in a moment like this? I translate everybody's fast English into slower English for my driver. He is careful with his pedals. He bobs his head in that graceful subconti-nental way. As soon as we're safely tucked onto the George Washington Bridge, I ask where he's from. *Bangladesh.* I've been there. *Twice,* I tell him. He turns his whole head around to look at me. Smiles. Every driver I've had in this city is from Pakistan, Palestine, Trinidad. It's a federation of brav-ery — the city's wheels steered by the wide world. *You saw my country?* he says brightly. *I saw it. I didn't drive there though. I didn't either,* he says. *I just got my first driver's license. Three months ago when I arrived here.*

We miss an exit. Actually, we miss a whole level of road. He says cheerfully, *Oh my goodness! We wanted to be up, but we are down.* Then he says, *The first time I was driving, someone wants to go to Newark Airport. I don't know it. I say where is it and they get very angry. They are shouting, Drive! Drive! They are telling me where to go. Actually that is what my company says — you only learn by going. When I leave them, I try to come back to New York City, but two hours later it is dark and a policeman by the side of road tells me I am going to Florida. Florida! Did you ever go to Florida? Pull over,* I say.

We roar into a gas station where I ask a lavishly tattooed man about Paterson and he tells me. Luckily there is not much traffic in our direction this morning. We are able to ease in and out of the flow. Now I am growing worried about my driver getting back into Manhattan with the horrendous traffic moving the other way. We pass houses with their eyes still shut, worlds we know not of and worlds we know too well. Kids with book bags. A thousand little turn-offs. Graffiti and pink trees. *Is it nice in Texas?* he asks me. *Very nice,* I say. *You could drive there. A lot.* Finally we pull up in front of a brick building in Paterson where I think I am supposed to be. Fifteen minutes early. *We made it!* He turns around to shake my hand a long time. *My friend!* he says, *We made it, yes we did! And I don't even know how to ride a bicycle!*

Learning the Language

One Word

Some days one word pleases the boy. He'll funnel it through his lips. He'll write it on small bits of paper that stick to the walls. He'll rub it, a candy on his tongue, so every other word tastes sweeter.

Echoes

In a house built by his great-grandparents, a man has trouble speaking. "Yes. I — redid it. Well, I tried — to do it — like they did it — first." In the mornings he washes his face with his grandmother's hands. She mutters, "Cluck – cluck – cluck" under her breath. His great-grandmother stands at the window staring out as the first few blades of grass poke up, the grass that will become a swooping green lawn by the end of the next century. It's the same as any story, adding onto itself, linking to others till barely a patch of brown shows through.

Eraser

I read poems in San Angelo, Texas. First I had to choose
which poems to read, the hard part. I had to think, "Some-
where out there is a person who might like to hear this."
Or, "On this day, this feels right." It's so strange how things
come up. It feels impossible. On the parking lot at the motel,
among pebbles and tar, an old button from a boy's Little
League uniform tried to give me advice.

Pulling out of the campus parking lot after the reading, I saw
a church marquee that said GOD HAS A BIG ERASER.
I could have felt grateful as it hit me over the head.

It's alright, I told myself. You'll feel better as you drive.
Almost like you left your voice behind you. Farms, fields,
stone-colored sheep. Mailbox at the rim of a huge cotton-
field, the family name lettered by hand: A.RIPPLE

Working for Tom

Again the truck labeled "TOM'S PEANUTS" swoops past at
a corner and I lean forward jealously to see the driver's face.
Across the city silver machines wait to be filled with peanuts,
candies, gums. When the truck empties, that driver gets to
go home, or loads another truck, but I cannot imagine him
always wandering, dreaming peanuts and peanut butters,
George Washington Carver's infinite variations. While I, in my
small house under the trees, seem to stay on the job all day
and night, sharpening pencils, wadding envelopes, clocking
the hours by occasional squirrel feet scrabbling across the roof.
Even while dreaming, I make a list of things to do, words to
contemplate: *radiant, stealth, help!* But the world is eating
peanuts. The world is happy with its simple life.

Second-to-Last Words

She says, I have left everything inside my house and when
I die, you will not find it there. You will not find it because
I have hidden it inside itself. Consider the day he held my
hand for a hundred miles. I never told anyone about this,
even who "he" was — they would have made something of it
much less than it was. He comforted me, but I would call it
political, not personal. Can you imagine anyone else seeing it
this way? If you discover my sewing kit tucked into its crack,
knot the blue silken thread, find something in your own life
coming loose. But don't assume that's how I held *my* needle.
Please, please water my plants. They are not "mine" exactly,
so they will not die with me. Read the stories whose pages I
have bent back in the magazines beside my bed. Then you
may throw them away. I had a few problems with that. I'm
not sure what will happen to the bed itself. I have given it
a map so it may follow me, away from here, from people
measuring days, but I don't really expect to meet it again. If
anyone wants to publish my letters, I leave that to you. Just
remember how I removed a wall in my studio to put win-
dows in. How there were many things I had not yet decided.

Rain Falling into the River
— That Moment as They Merge

In a cottage by a river, a man made stories. He lived so
fully in his room it was hard to get him out. His room grew
jungles, revising itself with light. I think he would stand in
his room staring out at rain falling into the river and wonder
why people went anywhere to begin with — this world of
avenues fashioning, tugging, offering what we learn to need
— he could see the sadness in that without even entering it.
Whole catalogues of sadness — species, radiant wings, and
eyes. He chose his quiet kind and planted banana leaf palms.
He drew little men who turn into donkeys. Little girls who
fly into flowers and sleep there. When people invited him to
come and talk to them about being an artist, he declined. It
was hard to talk to more than one person at a time, to say
the right words to enter so many ears at once. Better the
river's quiet pulse, the heaping mountains of cloud gathering
silently on any horizon, tilting the day a different way. He
drew a little boy and girl who wanted to be grown-up until
bedtime came — then they were ready to be small again.
Sometimes when I can't sleep I think of his pen in the room
next to the river, shaping, shaping, a jeweled crown, a kanga-
roo, a billowing tree. Since he died he's rewritten the whole
neighborhood.

His Life

I don't know what he thinks about. At night the vault of
his face closes up. He could be underground. He could be
buried treasure. He could be a donkey trapped in the Bisbee
Mine, lowered in so long ago with pulleys and belts, kicking,
till its soft fur faded and eyes went blind. They made don-
keys pull the little carts of ore from seam to seam. At night,
when the last men stepped into the creaking lift, the donkeys
cried. Some lived as long as 17 years down there. The min-
ers still feel bad about it. They would have hauled them out
to breathe real air in the evenings, but the chute was so deep
and they'd never be able to force them in again.

Editor-at-Large

A telephone message, "Call Loretta Belton as soon as you can," then the number. Her voice sounds urgent. Who is she? But she seems rather blasé when she picks up the phone. "Oh hi, do you remember when you visited my class about 20 years ago at Emerson Junior High? I gave you a big ol' manuscript of my poems to read and asked you to make comments on them? Which you did?" (I take a deep breath. Thank God. I thought she was about to say, "Where are they?") "Well anyway," she goes on, "I didn't take any of your advice. I mean, I read what you said, but I didn't change anything. I just put those poems away in a drawer. And now, for the first time in all these years, the manuscript surfaced. And I was wondering — do you think you could go over it again? I was thinking, maybe your ideas changed."

Nothing Big Enough

The obituary column of the local newspaper has started a new fashion of reporting people's deaths; each day, a few newly dead ones get "featured" with headlined stories, photos, quotes from family and friends. Rarely do the closest kin do the talking — usually it's a nattering cousin or neighbor ready to tell. The headlines seem peculiarly reductive: JOE MONTOYA ONCE CAMPED AT TERLINGUA, SARAH BERKMAN ENJOYED PICKLE MAKING, RUDY RIOS LOVED 1965 CHEVROLET. Even headlines which attempt to span decades or describe sensibilities — GLADYS ROBERTS VALUED INDEPENDENCE — don't seem big enough. Is that *it*? Is that what *they* would have chosen to say? I think of a summer when my neighbor Susie and I became obsessed with cold noodle salads, driving to the rim of the city to purchase fresh pasta, trading recipes, clipping basil from one another's yards. We haven't done anything together since. What if I died and they asked her about me? Would she say, "Angel hair," nodding gravely? Never once had I imagined my own mother dreamed of flying up in a hot-air balloon till she called last week to describe it. Forget the tidbits — they're not fair. At least at the end. There's no room for rebuttal — "I did *not* like butternut squash the best." Better the note my friend's father left stuck to her screen door — "I'm not here anymore" — before driving home to die.

Monticello, Montpelier, Mount Vernon

We are so full of presidents we simply must sit down and eat.
"Stafford's Home Cooking" has blue and white checkered
curtains in the windows. I am in the mood grown-ups get
into when they have done too many things in quick succes-
sion. My son, whose head is not throbbing, was fascinated
by the death story of George Washington. "What do you
mean," he asked the guide, as we all gazed at the canopied
bed in which George died, "his throat closed up? Couldn't
he cough to open it? Does that disease still exist today?"

I preferred yesterday, hearing how James Madison turned his
face away from his last bowl of oatmeal. When asked, "Has
something happened?" he replied simply, "Nothing but a
change of mind," and died later that morning.

The sloppy menu at Stafford's is handwritten and stained.
Marginal notes declare, "Thank you, Jesus! We love you,
God!" Does God eat here? Obviously we have stumbled
into an evangelical enterprise. The waiter, a thick young
man wearing a rumpled white shirt, appears fairly ho-hum. I
motion him over. "Tell me something," I say, popping two
Nuprins. "Is your catfish that lumpy frozen-morsels kind or
real genuine catfish?" He grows visibly excited. "Oh ma'am,
it's the real good kind, straight from a lake, we grow it our-
selves, I promise, you can count on it." I begin counting. My
son orders grilled cheese, an item on which he has become
expert, coast-to-coast. We rearrange salt shakers, argue about
air-conditioning. I do not like a direct draft. My son would
sit inside the cooler itself if they let him. Behind the dan-
gling implements and fry pans visible through the swinging

kitchen door, the pulse of a miracle hides. Someone has been altered, saved, swept away. Someone was sick and got well. I want to know what happened here. My historical mood demands it. I study the menu more closely. Between the macaroni casserole and the stuffed cabbages, the baked potatoes and stroganoffs, a repeatedly urgent chorus … JESUS IS THE KEY TO LIFE! BELIEVE!!!!!!!! But my smudged copy, fastened askew, inserted crookedly in its own cover, reads: JESUS IS THE KEY TO   Catfish.

Birds in Breath

Dying, he watched birds at two feeders just beyond his window. Dip and swoop. Balancing dance as plump dove tipped feeder askew for tiny finch. Busy. Grip of bird claw inside his skin. And what was thrown aside? Shell, shell and grit. You could count on it, birds swirling. He felt soft after so much night. Later they would rest. There wouldn't be any eating. Wind at feeders. Later. Breath lost. Hard to. Pull it in anymore. And he used to sing and say, anything. Used to make those students sit up, startled. Feeling the fluttering crawl inside their mouths. Letting the songs go. Out.

How They Come Back into Our Lives

Late at night. Collect. With a stereo turned up loud.
Suddenly needing to be woven together, young, or re-
membered. Needing someone else besides whatever they
have become. *Is the door open? Do you recall four feathers*
pointing four directions, how we planned to travel every way
at once? What happened? I'm still here. Listen, you must look
just the same. I don't. Things were good but they got shaky.
I'm standing on the street in front of Buster's Tattoo Parlor.
I may have to sleep here. Have you ever been inside a tattoo
parlor in your life? What's your address? I keep losing it.
I wrote you a letter when we had a giant electrical storm two
years ago. Thunder all night nonstop. Remember my father's
voice? It's here somewhere.

Sunday Newspaper

Our Nation's Capital

Before we even cross the river, the taxi driver tells how
many people were murdered here last night. I lean for-
ward, trying to pinpoint his accent, deciding not to bring
it up. He roars wildly through a red signal. "You been here
before? Business or pleasure?" He says it used to be bad
but not this bad.

Familiar glimpses of monuments I have never entered.
Even the Smithsonian — I have this feeling if I go in there
I won't come out. Dinosaurs moving their mouths.

Inside my hotel room the bedspread has been removed,
sheets turned down. A green mint balanced on the pillow.
Soft light. A basket of creamy herbal lotions and soaps by
the sink.

All night emergency vehicles race by outside, wailing and
blinking. In the morning a newspaper rich with disasters
will be resting outside each door. We brush our teeth. We
feel at home.

Pictures from the Village

Your faces carry a different light. Because the soldiers poke you in the backs with their guns, because you have worried your whole lives long about every inch, every step, every child, every tree. What gets better? Year to year. The Israelis say they are sick of you. They say it to your faces. Your house is 200 years old and they act like you just arrived. *How many stones do they have over there anyway?* asks an American, reading the newspaper. The major crop. Quiet shine. Undersides of leaves, veined and ripe. Intricate traceries of labor. Steady gaze of constellations, radiating in place, whether or not we give them names.

Sunday Newspaper, August 6

Today the comics should not be on top. Not folded first
under the rubber band as for a day of primary colors, bouncy
talk. There should be no *Entertainment News,* no *TV Guide,*
no ads. Today a great silence should walk around the edges
of the words on every page and not let us use words again
until we remember to be changed.

Why the Silence Still Hangs
Over Eastern Oregon

In the photograph, one shoulder of Chief Young Joseph
droops lower than the other. "Due to a childhood injury
falling from a horse." (Maybe.) An interpreter kneels beside
him as a woman in a wide skirt conveys bad news. I hope
the words hurt her throat. Did they send a woman to make
the message seem gentler? I hope her whole tongue scalded
and burned. Chief Young Joseph, who had grown up with
talkative rivers, deep valleys, green mountains wearing cloud-
caps, had to tell his people next. He had to tell them. No
picture of that moment. White tipis at Wallowa shine in the
lake's dark eyes. To this day it is impossible to gaze easily into
that water. Chief Young Joseph did not like Kansas one bit.
He said, "I think very little of this country."

What Has Been Done To Women

Yesterday you cried in the car when you said soldiers in that war asked if women were fair game and the leaders said, "Yes, fair game, do anything you want to them." My own throat filled up when you said the woman you are loving now asks you please to say more sweet things to her. We passed battered barns and bushes, every license plate said OREGON in one color or another, we passed the rest stop planted with trees of all the 50 United States. The really hot sunny states were having trouble. Access roads and overpasses, stores selling all manner of useless things. I watched the seam of your cheek as you spoke, we named people we had loved that the other would never know, they were clues to the road. We talked about the ugly words hurled at women for centuries, how they all have a click-shut sound, and why is it some lives feel hard as a curb that you kick. And how could they be softened. I told you about Coleman, on the night he was robbed, saying, "How long do you stay robbed once you've been robbed? I think I'm getting over it" — and Susan, later, translating "robbed" into "raped" and weeping with joy — how long it takes any body to get over, get under, get out, shout.

Heirs

What skin we must develop to read the newspaper and not
split wide open. The boy named Ray is found floating in
the river. Ray had a gleaming face and a nine-year-old hope.
We see him smiling many days in a row. What did he sing
inside his head as he flew to our city to visit his father? Was
he proud? His father had paid no attention to him during
the early years, but recently decided to "act like a dad." The
dad's girlfriend reports the beatings started soon after Ray
arrived in Texas. Dad took him into the back room. Dad had
the same name as his own dad who once killed a Chinese
grocer's son. The same name as his grandfather who now
sits on his porch wondering what the hell "happened to his
heirs." Ray is described as a "nice kid." We hear much more
about his father. Ray was on the honor roll. He's in all our
families now.

Mistakes

Behind us our mistakes shine brilliantly, torches that could guide us every direction, if only we could turn around.

Once in the Rothko Chapel, past and future swam together, equally, resiliently black – and such a sweet, small thing to move between them. What, beyond that, could ever take our hands?

Grace, because I wouldn't pour you the 27th glass of milk before you walked out the door to fly to Australia, I have to keep pouring it until you return.

Sometimes on the darkest trails – cursing, mud swallowing shoes – an avocado tree looms, dangling its pear-shaped bounty, utterly above reach. On the ground, a shell of avocado, pulp dug out by some hiker in time for the last low one. You feel glad for that person in a morose kind of way. You don't even care about the waterfall at the end of this trail. Surely the person who ate the avocado will be there, floating in the pool at the bottom, a secretly pleased expression on his face, though the guidebook says, *Beware of falling rocks.* He's used to being lucky. It also says, *Watch for tangled roots every second. If you lose concentration, your ankle can snap.* So what kind of trail is this? Watching the ground instead of the mountains and trees? But it's too confusing. Wouldn't giving up and turning around be a bigger mistake?

Trudging back from the waterfall, the mud feels slicker, twice as deep. At first you worried about keeping your shoes clean, now you're thinking about your shirt. And you know, just as the hardest rain starts penetrating the leaves, this swimmer will come leaping past you in his boxer shorts, barefoot, staring straight ahead.

Hammer and Nail

"Would you like to see where our little girl is buried?" my friend asks as we walk between stucco shrines and wreaths of brilliant flowers. Even a plane's propeller is attached to a pilot's grave as if the whole thing might spin off into the wind. One man's relatives built a castle over his remains, with turrets and towers, to match the castle he built for his body in life. If you stand at a certain angle you can see both castles at once, the bigger one he lived in off on the horizon. An archway says in Spanish, "Life is an illusion. Death is the reality. Respect the dead whom you are visiting now." We hike down the hill toward the acres of "free graves." Here people can claim any space they want without paying, but also risk having someone buried on top of them. In the fields beyond the cemetery, women walk slowly with buckets slung over their shoulders on poles. My friend kneels. The cross-bar from the marker of her child's grave has come loose and lies off to one side. She presses the simple blue crossbar back into the upright piece, wishing for a hammer and nail. The cross has delicate scalloped edges and says nothing. No words, no dates. It reminds me of the simplicity of folded hands, though I know there were years of despair. My friend says, "Sometimes I am still very sad. But I no longer ask, 'What if … ?' It was the tiniest casket you ever saw." On the small plots in either direction, families have stuck tall pine branches into dirt. The needles droop, completely dried by now, but they must have looked lovely as miniature forests for the first few days.

Dallas Suburban

We grew lonely for birds in that house surrounded by eight-foot fences and wedges of terrace. We slept in a room for guests. Where was the music that used to pull us out of bed into a day? Only sounds of our own species: a banging door, a distant engine roaring. When people spoke together, their words circled what was in sight. Once I caught a slim trail of chirrup beyond the massive Tudor towers poking up side-by-side but couldn't find it again in that well-divided air.

The Endurance of Poth, Texas

It's hard to know how well a town is when you only swing
through it on suspended Sunday evenings maybe twice a
year. Deserted streets. The dusty faces of stores: elderly aunts
with clamped mouths. I like to think Monday morning still
buzzes and whirls — rounded black autos roll in from farms,
women measure yard goods, boys haul empty bottles to the
grocery, jingling their coins. Nothing dries up. I want towns
like Poth and Panna Maria and Skidmore to continue forever
in the flush, red-cheeked, in love with all the small comings
and goings of cotton trucks, haylifts, peaches, squash, the
cheerleader's sleek ankles, the young farmer's nicked ear.
Because if they don't, what about us in the cities, those gray
silhouettes off on the horizon? We're doomed.

Living Alone Inside One's Own Body

Some days light falls in warm sheets. The metallic gray sky
seems reflective — I know that weather. Fear takes on a fa-
miliar taste. Even regret, that stone, that peach pit turned on
the tongue. And the man raking next door before dawn —
how can he see what he is raking? I like the sound of bricks
being stacked, the heavy clink. I like the dragging grate of his
rake's teeth through wet, dark leaves.

Trade

I took Nuala to the village to meet my Sitti, age 105, sitting up inside the white sheets of her bed. Nuala wanted to know how to say *Hello* and *Thank You* in Arabic, she wrote it down in her notebook before we got there. *Marhaba*, Nuala said, and my Sitti said, "Who's that?" Everyone said, "She's pretty." Sitti said, "Does she have a husband? Does she have a child?" Nuala said, "I'd take a child." Outside, soldiers were pounding the streets with the butts of their guns. My relatives didn't see them anymore. "They're invisible." The walls said NO! NO! NO! But Muhammad wore his Happy Life T-shirt. Nuala said, "I have a grandmother too. She's 100. She's sitting in her bed on the coast of Ireland right now, staring out to sea." And my Sitti eating pralines from Texas said in Arabic, "Do you think she'd trade places with me?"

Off

Each time she opened her mouth, a small room of air fell out. And recently, following each word, a winged surge of regret. Those gulls that trace a tractor's furrows in a field? What's planted here? What's being planted?

Sometimes in the middle of conversations one gull flew off alone, back toward where he imagined the sea, while the rest of them were busy.

Brazen

A young French couple traveling Nepal with their large dog invited me to join them for a day-long hike. Passing a rural homestead on a steep slope, we paused for water and their dog lunged after a white chicken, chased it in a wild flurry of squawking, bit down hard on its back, and began to eat it. The Frenchman stood without moving. His wife waved her hands. The chicken's owners appeared from behind the house looking confused, carrying a bucket and a shovel. I hoped this wasn't the only chicken they owned. Hopefully other chickens nested in secret places at that very moment, laying many extra eggs. The Frenchman calmly plucked a fistful of rupees from his pocket and handed them over to the woman with the bucket. I felt enormous in my down jacket. The dog wore feathers stuck to his face the rest of the day. We walked silently for a long time through brilliant scenery and we were not staying.

El Paso Sky

When it's no good on earth I look up. When the cups on my
table all have chips around the edges and I can't get that feel-
ing of what to do next, I press my eyes into the skinny pink
stripe melting under the blue rumple that rolls and rolls and
the dark corner growing over the mountains. I say to myself,
"It's happening without you." If I had the biggest arms in
the world, I couldn't hug that. When I think of the people
who are dead now, who weren't dead just a little while ago,
and how easy it would have been to pick up the phone and
talk to them by dialing a number — I look at the sky. It's all
one piece now.

Appetite

All Intermediate Points

If today you are going to Buda, Texas and the bus rolls into Buda, Texas and stops, you climb down and you are ready to climb down. Perhaps you sigh, make a great heave-ho. It has been a long trip. But if today you are going to St. Louis or Pittsburgh and the bus passes through Buda, Texas and someone else climbs down, it does not seem like a long trip at all. This has always fascinated me. And if you are sitting in a bus terminal and the muddled loudspeaker announces ALL ABOARD FOR DEL RIO AND EL PASO AND ALL IN-TERMEDIATE POINTS, does the phrase "all intermediate points" wash over you pungently as the scent of bus terminal hotcakes and do you eat them one at a time?

Future

When she wrote from the shores of Puget Sound to say
she had burned all her poems since that workshop we had
together 10 years ago *but had I by chance saved anything she
wrote because now she would like to look at it* something thud-
ded inside me. The sound of an apple dropping into soft
grass at the base of a tree. Not even a big wind. She had said
emphatically to our group, *We should get rid of everything
we do because only then can we move into the future,* and I
said simply, *Nonsense,* while other people talked a long time
one way or another about her advice. That day the feel-
ing of belonging nowhere seemed very close. Not with the
people, not with anybody's idea of anything, nor with the
deer I had seen stepping gingerly over a heap of fallen fence.
Where were *they* going? Staring past our circle into the sky
that had done nothing since the beginning of time but hold
first one weather then another, I tried to think of a question
to ask her. The clouds had teeth and tails. They were roil-
ing up from one horizon, glowing in the center of the sky,
dissolving on the other side. *Why not just a good box? And
what about the single line that will rise up from a troubled page
years later like a little stick you could hold onto?* Someone rang
the dinner gong. We were eating lots of salads at that camp.
I thought everyone was kissing when I couldn't see them.
They all had leaves in their hair. Where did the future begin?
In our cabin we found postcards to Aunt Maggie in a drawer.
More than 70 years old, they urged her to have a good time,
to remember everybody back home who wished they could
be with her, high up over the river, biting into bread with a
hard crust, guzzling air.

Appetite

Focaccia, fougasse, the bread aisle swims with warm syllables, yeasty dough of names, rosemary sticks, bialy, Afghani bread — as if by saying we could bring ourselves back from the wars — *challah, pita, tortilla,* each bin a universe of dark eyes, glint of olive oil, brushed onions, bread in knots, studded raisins I raise to my lips. Which part of us is always hungry? My friends turning 40 this year who call late to say — What next? — are with me here, and Mr. Laguna with his two teeth, his life after 90 that only waits. Pumpernickel, please. Don't make me move on.

40's

MIDDLE, as in AGE, as in CHILD, has a dismal, dirty ring.
Why? Pressed in. Shouldn't it be the sweetest part of the
cake? I drove through the middle of Syracuse and never saw
it, it was snowing so hard. Should I go back there? People
with set lips? Forget them.

Island

All the envelopes on the desk are bleaching quietly, swallowing their own addresses, forgetting where they came from. At night they fly out the windows, circle the house and scoot back in through the louvres. That's why they're lying in a pile when we wake up. It's hard to remember the big land connected to other land. It's hard to remember who wrote this, if anyone answered. See that little sail way off by the line where sea and sky get together? It's a letter. It's to all of us. That's the happiest line in the world.

Bingo!

We've paid $3.50 each for four hard cards but then a man with a big belly drifts around the room selling paper ones too. *More cards ya have, better chance ta win.* He pokes us twice with that line so of course one dollar follows another and soon it's hard to keep track of all our rows. We left this room 15 years ago and never returned till now. No one here has given up smoking yet. We peer through the haze. Our cards set up on scarred wooden racks. At halftime the old man across from me cuts his slab of pineapple cake. He is sipping coffee from a 100-year-old cup. *Have you won recently?* I ask and he shakes his head *no* so slowly the two moth holes in the brim of his hat barely wobble. His cigar stub rests in the saucer. It's obvious we're not regulars since we're the only ones who remark when we get anything. The man who calls out the numbers sits on a stage with a lit board and a microphone. He has power. To be IN the BIN with digits, to invoke the 57 — my daddy doesn't even see when he has a line-up right in front of him. Luckily the man with the belly is leaning over his shoulder at that very moment and shouts out *Bingo!* for him as if he never learned English yet and the man runs up front with the winning card while my daddy says *It is? It really is?* and the man comes back to poke a 10-dollar bill into his startled hand. *Sure it is! Thass a good little ol' bingo!* Then of course we all think we may have missed a win and scan our cards with deeper concentration but nobody else wins anything all night at our whole table even the waitress next to me who comes here every single Friday and has to take three buses to get home.

Shrine of Hair

It stands or falls according to its morning whim. He grips the comb. Bites his lip staring into an antique mirror that makes every face look wider than it really is. He's furious at how fast hair grows. Doesn't it know he wants it to be short and stiff standing up like a small wall in front in the style of some Latino singing star? Instead it bends or separates, slouching to the right. Then there is the issue of school, the coming trapped hours, while the lucky cat lounges on the step all day, licking and licking his own gray sheen.

Library Card

Someone has forged my library card. The second me favors philosophy, aesthetics, theories of evolution. We evolve into people who are not ourselves. The impostor is smarter than I am. The impostor likes checking out better than returning. But we have our own troubles. Eighteen lost books from the children's department turn up in an ice chest in our shed, nine months later. They are well-cooled and rested. How big can a fine be? The library will try to intercept the impostor at the check-out desk. Will ask her to name my birthday. Aha! *Someone without an address of her own borrowed yours.* How many things we haven't thought of yet. *Someone* is every-where. We share periodicals, elevators, bathrooms. A glimpse into gloom and the quickly-turned head. Someone drinking out of the hose in my front yard. Think what a book offers otherwise. *Never mind. Shall I foot your bill? Don't be gone — read on. What better thing to do?* (March 12, 1952)

Magnetic Poetry Kit

I'm more interested in words that fall off the refrigerator door by themselves than the lanky lines we make.

urge

Alone, on a red tile, in a little pool of light.

Bright Needle Poked through Dark Cloth

Light arriving in villages, lifting stone, opening shadows, a girl finds a circle of light on her hand. Even the broom in its corner, soles of shoes jumbled on the doorstep, a book left open till it blinks inside a film of dust — without morning did not belong to one another. Did not remember how they were invented or touched.

Birthday Present

On the evening of the day our son turned five, Mars, Jupiter, and Venus gathered in the closest heavenly configuration since 1716. Cuddled up in a little triangle of sky, three pinpricks of light, two brilliant, Mars dimmer but holding its place, and we told the story of how little he'd been, a cat, a tucked-up chicken with a white cap on its head. "Five years ago I was born," he said, in a voice clear as a radio announcer, absolute as a czar. It interested him less that the planets had massed, that the neighbors left their homemade ice cream freezers to stand in the street looking up. "Now tell me about six. What was I doing six years ago?" So we spun the mysteries in our dark palms before him; once we didn't know each other, any of us. Once we had no bodies, we were floating out there, maybe, in that dark place between points. Once nobody called us by any name and we never came. Once, once, the door opening a million stories, the leap into skin, into stars, planets people could point at confidently from thousands of miles away to say, "There they are."

Fairbanks

This much sun keeps us awake, walking outside. At midnight you grew a shadow 20 feet tall. You kept spinning the long thread of a story around your finger — how they got here — how these people came to live among bears, wolves — one would have to be *seized*. Yesterday which could have been today the way they run together, a woman shrilled at us, "Notice our light is HORIZONTAL, not VERTICAL like that awful pounding sun you have in Texas" — obviously mad at someone who once made her live in Texas — but also right. The day spread out horizontally around our heads. They swear these trees were bare a moment ago — so much sun frills birches out double-speed. Carrots swell to giants in the Matanuska Valley. We imagine lives twice as large as lives back home. Forgetting, for a moment, winter, that extended drone whose compensation, the aurora, pulls people outside. Nancy swears she lies on her back at 30 below because beauty is bigger than cold. I'd like to see it. I'd like to bend till the rest of my years take on these strange stretched lines. Buds bubble from sticks, fat clouds of mosquitoes swarm our skins, too lazy to bite. And the long leaves of shining days remind me of the softness sometimes after being sick, when we open doors gingerly and step out blinking, as if light carried us here and slid us down again altered, unsure just how.

Paris

Once my father and I were flying home from the Middle East and we stopped in Paris for 24 hours. Our taxi driver told us what happiness was. "It's when you don't want anything. You don't hate it, you just don't want it. You like it, in fact. You just don't want it." I told him he sounded like a Buddhist, but he didn't want that either. He said nobody in Paris was happy. He let us off on a street where vendors sold cream puffs and hosiery and snazzy yellow-toed shoes and pears and fresh baguettes and wine. The whole day and night I was in Paris, I bought nothing. Not one thing. Not even a postcard. At the restaurant I asked the waitress to choose for me, partly because I couldn't read French, but also because I wasn't sure what I wanted. We could have changed our tickets and stayed 10 days. My father wanted to. I could have bought Parisian socks, a tin of lemon drops. My father kept shaking his head, asking, "What's the rush?" He told me I'd be sorry later. It wasn't the first time he'd predicted this. But I felt happy in Paris, so briefly, breezing up and down those streets I'd never know with my empty hands.

Humility

Rick, the carpenter who built our gate, appears at the door. "Look what I found," he says, dangling my first long-out-of-print book of poems. At a garage sale in his neighborhood. In a box of loose plumbing parts, those rubber domes that go in the backs of toilets. Marked one dollar. He hands over the book for me to sign. "Give you two dollars," I say, and he shakes his head. "Finders, keepers." Then I ask if they were selling lots of books and he says, "No, only yours."

This Is My Solemn Vow

1

To their credit, the bride and groom recite the famous
lines from memory instead of repeating them. *Richer
or poorer, better or worse* ... Were the rest of us dunces
or what? But the bride has to be prompted on her last
line, which causes her to burst out laughing. Since
all four parents of bride and groom are divorced and
remarried, the front row is quite full. *Welcome,* said the
vicar, *Family and friends, Family and friends, Family
and friends* ... did they also make a solemn vow more
than once and laugh and if not, should they have?

2

Vows: not to talk too much. To remain unobtrusive as
possible. Not to fly off the handle. To find the handle.
To grip it tightly. Not to make anybody feel more
uncomfortable in the world than they already do. Who?
We are more solemn than stones. Not to pile my desk.
But being solemn also *weighs,* like a sky that refuses to
rain after smoldering for days.

3

USE WHAT YOU HAVE says the sign on my wall,
so I won't buy any clothes for four years maybe five.
Already one year and six months have passed and I feel
richer than when I started, not so much in money, but
in clothes and in friends. Women bring clothes they
don't want anymore to my back porch, we have gi-
ant trades. Surrounding ourselves with baggy linens,
jackets, velvet vests, we draw numbers, poke our arms

through each other's sleeves. We have grown muscular, more reckless. I am the only person, they vote, who would ever wear that checkered jacket. Susie takes my Turkish shoes. Who are we now as opposed to all those earlier selves? I vow to find out. The life of poetry pins us to the minute. Do we fit?

Epilogue

Mint Snowball II

I passed through Shelbyville, Illinois a few days ago for the first time in 35 years, the town where my great-grandfather had his drugstore and made his mint snowballs. I walked up and down the main street, happy the town seemed to be thriving – no boards over shop windows. Upbeat, old-fashioned, lovely. I went to my great-grandparent's old house and talked to the man who lives there now. Within three minutes of my arrival, he said, "You know what I will never forget in my whole life?" (He is 70) "The taste of that mint snowball your great-grandfather used to make."

I almost fainted on the grass ... "And how old were you when you had it?" He said, "Between the ages of five and ten – my mom used to get it for me when I was good."

About the Author

Born of a Palestinian father and an American mother,
Naomi Shihab Nye grew up in St. Louis, Jerusalem and
San Antonio, where she graduated from Trinity University.
She still lives a block from the San Antonio River, with her
husband, photographer Michael Nye and their son. She has
worked widely as a visiting writer.

Nye is the author of seven poetry collections and a number
of award-winning books for young readers. She is featured
on two PBS documentaries, *The Language of Life* with Bill
Moyers, and *The United States of Poetry*. She has received a
Guggenheim Fellowship, two Jane Addams Children's Book
Awards and the Witter Bynner Fellowship from the Library
of Congress. She is also the poetry editor for *The Texas
Observer*. She traveled abroad on three Arts America tours
sponsored by the United States Information Agency.